Muddy Moos and Midges

by

Sue Wood

Printed in the United Kingdom

First Printing, 2021

Published by KDP

For Robyn and Erika

Morag's wellies started to squeak

It began on Monday, the start of the week.

A large family of mice,

Found them cosy and nice.

Morag cried, "Eek-Eek-Eek"!

Giggly, Giggly Woolly-Skye,

Giggled so much until she cried.

She giggled all day,

She giggled all night.

Giggly, Giggly Woolly-Skye.

Effie's byre was cluttered with stuff,

Boxes and beds and bags full of fluff.

She added more and more,

Now she could not close the door.

"No-No-No… enough is enough!"

Dotty's pig is greedy as can be,

Her favourite word is, "me-me-me"

She gobbles all the food,

Which is very, very rude.

Dotty's pig is now round as can be.

Little Red-Fergie was a friendly chap,

With four black tyres and a diesel cap.

He stayed in the barn,

Which was cosy and warm.

His engine started with a tap, tap, tap.

Cocky-Cockerel diddley-ding,

Flapping around with a bee on his wing.

Jumping up high

And dropping down low.

Cocky-Cockerel diddley-ding.

Hector's hen with the pointy beak,

Ate his flowers at the start of the week.

Hector planted many more,

Such a long and boring chore.

Hector cried, "Oh what a cheek!"

Fisherman Tam sat in the sun.

Eating his favourite cheese and ham bun.

A seagull flew by,

With a glint in her eye.

Snatched Tam's bun - just for fun.

Highland coo lived on the hill,

Complained each day that, she was ill.

She fell into a pool,

Which was ever so cool.

Poor soggy-wet moo on the hill.

The windy-wind blew up in a storm

And blew Meg's sheets and pants on the lawn.

They were covered in mud,

Which wasn't very good

Meg shook her fist at the storm.

Angy-Angus was digging the peat.

He stacked them up in a nice neat heap.

He was itchy and warm,

In a huge midge swarm.

Angy-Angus ran home for a sleep.

Harry Haggis is round as can be,

His legs are hairy and very wee.

He rolled down the hill,

Which made him feel ill.

As he rolled, he cried, "we-e-e-e...!"

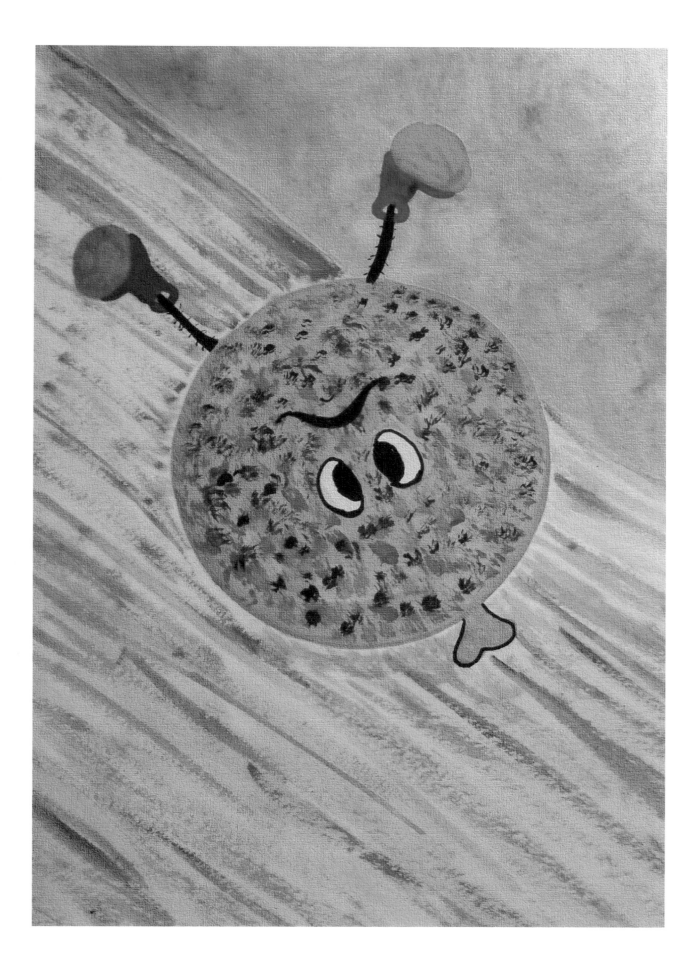

Shepherd Seamus fell fast asleep,

When he woke up, he'd lost his sheep.

He searched up the glen

And down on the shore.

Shepherd Seamus has found his sheep.

Down on the croft are lambs and sheep,

Chickens, tatties and rows of neeps.

With rushes and reeds,

Wildflowers and seeds.

Dig-dig-dig and stack peats in a heap.

Midge Mac, loves to attack.

She bites your arms, bottom and your back.

She loves to drink blood,

Which is not very good.

Midge Mac loves to attack.

The crafty fox is out tonight,

Rabbits and mice will get a fright.

He is ever so quick,

Never misses a trick.

All the animals keep out of sight.

Hamish the ram with the curly horns,

Ate all the grass on Betty's lawn.

He was whooshed through the gate,

At a lightening rate.

He ran next door onto Mary's lawn.

Haggis, neeps and tatties yum, yum, yum!

Filling up my empty tum.

Hate them or love them!

Love them or hate them!

Haggis, neeps and tatties yum, yum, yum!

About the Author Sue Wood

Sue has lived on the Isle of Skye working with pre-school children for over 26 years. She has a passion for children's books and has read thousands of stories during her career spanning over forty years. A retired early years lecturer with University of Highlands and Islands, Sue still works part time with young children. Sue now spends most of her time writing poetry, painting and enjoying nature.

Muddy Moos and Midges was written to support children and young people's mental health.

Printed in Great Britain
by Amazon